Become a Leader with Authority
Your Success Toward a Legacy

Silver Anniversary Series

By David K. Ewen, M.Ed.

Copyright © 2018, 2019

Ewen Prime Company

All rights reserved. No part of this publication may be reproduced, distributed, or transmitted in any form or by any means, including photocopying, recording, or other electronic or mechanical methods, without the prior written permission of the publisher, except in the case of brief quotations embodied in critical reviews and certain other noncommercial uses permitted by copyright law.

ISBN-13: 978-1718636378

ISBN-10: 1718636377

2 - Become a Leader with Authority - 2

About the book

There are many books and discussions about what leadership is. This book talks about how it is developed and what the purpose is through a person's life. By understanding the purpose of leadership, motivation is produced that lends itself to put people into the role of leadership. A leader can be a parent, a coach, a pastor, business owner, teacher, mentor, etc. This book gives insight and revelation to the power of leadership Behavior in a person's life to make them more effective so that they could leave a legacy behind in the world they live in before they go to heaven. Effective leadership gives purpose and meaning to life. Do it right and you'll be satisfied with having a purpose and honored for having a legacy.

4 - Become a Leader with Authority - 4

Style of Book

This book was written as a narrative discussion as part of a lecture. This supports the silver anniversary series of Ewen Prime Company and is part of the celebration the topic of leadership is presented as in identifying factor of the success of the company.

About the Author

David K. Ewen, M.Ed. Is an author, speaker, talk show host, publisher, and entrepreneur. He has been seen internationally at education venues and institutions helping youth and adults maximize their potential through teaching and lectures. David is the founder of the Boston Institute for Business Leaders and Entrepreneurs.

7 - Become a Leader with Authority - **7**

David K. Ewen, M.Ed.

The first lesson I got in leadership came from my father when I was a little boy. He told me that the difference between a man and a boy is that the man does what they have to do and the boy does want to do. As he described as he was talking about responsibility.

The second lesson I got in leadership came from myself through my failures. I learned the hard way what being responsible was by doing the opposite. This way I could learn firsthand difference between a man and a boy. I learned that by doing what I wanted to do instead of what I have to do is not responsible. My actions were able to prove that the first lesson I learned in leadership by my father was correct.

After the first and second lesson my next lesson in leadership came from observation so that I could see the difference between a man and a boy as my father had described. By observing the outside world I was able to see success and failure. My father taught by example in demonstration through his daily Behavior and that served as the foundation of my understanding of leadership.

My father had a doctorate in physics after having discovered hydrogen in space and lunching the industry and studies of radio astronomy at Harvard University. His role in science in the area of providing a contribution to an industry and a field of science served as one observation of leadership that I could see first aunt.

I remember as a little boy my parents had corporate parties for my father's business. My mother would hand me a paper plate that I could play with as a frisbee as I ran in between all of my father's colleagues and employees. Even as a boy I could see how our special visitors attending the evening barbecue looked up to my father. I observed the respect and honor that he received. Somehow, I knew that the respect and honor was earned and not given freely. I'm not sure how I knew that, but I knew that something special happened for that respect and honor to be bestowed upon him.

Although I observed it as a little boy, be understanding of earning respect and honor rather than receiving it would be learned and understood years later. That understanding would come through trial and error and trudging through mistake to recognize that leaders earn respect because of their behavior and actions. Fortunately, I learned that a title or position comes with responsibility. My understanding of responsibility came from that very first lesson my father gave me about the difference between a man and a boy. Children inherently want to grow up such as myself wanting to go from a boy to a man therefore taking on responsibility.

Education and the path towards graduation can teach people about leadership and the responsibility that comes with it. A certificate or diploma with a degree is earned and not given. I tell people I earned my master's degree in education (M.Ed.) . I didn't get my masters degree. There was a lot of hard work to earn my degree.

It was during the process of earning a masters degree that I learn responsibility involved sacrifice. Many enjoyable things had to be put on hold while I pursued earning my master's degree. During my undergraduate studies I was a full-time student and worked part-time occasionally. But it was during my Graduate Studies when I was working full-time during the day and pursuing my graduate studies at night and during the weekends. Both full time ventures would not offer the opportunity for recreational fun. This is an example of sacrifice.

Up to now my lessons in leadership involved first understanding responsibility from my father and then sacrifice during my Graduate Studies as I pursued my master's degree in education full time working full-time. By the time I walked up on stage and received my master's degree. I had already learned my first two lessons in leadership. They were responsibility and sacrifice.

After having learned my first two lessons in leadership in the area of responsibility and sacrifice, it was time to learn my next lesson in leadership. A full-time can only be interesting if there's an evolution of progress during the life of the career. The interest is lost if the career is stagnant meaning that there is no opportunity for promotion or that higher level of excitement on the job by doing more interesting things. I learned that the more interesting assignments in my computer data processing profession would only come if I accepted a lead role in projects that required organization of tasks and schedule. This means time management. My next lesson in leadership had to do with time management specifically in the area of mastering a schedule of tasks and organizing it in a way that the timeline of the project was optimized.

As I was learning time management in an area of schedule and ordering tasks, I stumbled. The way I stumbled was by rushing certain Milestones of a project which caused some failure along the way. My next lesson in leadership came from those failures. I learned that failure did not produce success. Time management could not be successful if there was failure in even just one milestone. I learned that and optimized use of time would only be worth it if and only if the tasks were done with excellence. My next lesson in leadership had to do with excellence. I remember a boss that I had at a workplace told me that the one thing you do not check is what will fail. Checking and dub king a few things and not all things will still result in failure. I learned to accept that the one thing that I did not check will fail because the prevention of that failure required a double check. Anything that did not have a double check would sale. The time to double-check had to be included in my optimize schedule as part of time management. The process of checking and verification had to be included and embedded in the schedule. Excellence it's a process. The process of Excellence is the attention to detail and that attention is a focus on all aspects of what is being performed.

Leadership involves working with people and to do that you have to meet with people. Being late to a meeting prevent that from happening. My next lesson in leadership had to do with the time management specifically with meeting people on time. That lesson was in commitment. The understanding of commitment is an understanding of behavior and actions you do with other people. To maximize my commitment to the collaboration with other people I ensured to the best of my ability that I was not late at the assigned meeting time. To guarantee that I was not late I accept it the extra time incurred upon me to be early. That extra time would be embedded in my process of time management. That means commitment requires time management skills. It is necessary to account for the time it takes to be on time and that effort involves commitment.

To guarantee the committee of being on time is to anticipate the obstacles that can delay and arrival that would prevent being on time. My next lesson in leadership is related to anticipation. The anticipation of anything that can prevent success are the things that must be included in a timeline of an effort that needs to be done. Anticipation is a responsibility if commitment is to be successful. An example is on the day of my wedding when it almost rained and could comment a late arrival to the place of ceremony for my wife and I. As part of tradition we both arrived separately and early. We both independently anticipated that rain could cause a delay in travel and made Provisions so that we would not arrive late. We did so to commit being on time to show courtesy and respect to our visitors who would be standing outside. Although there were like sprinkles on that day, not rain so the wedding was held outside as originally planned. But it was on that day that my wife and I independently exercise leadership in the area of anticipation and commitment.

Most companies I work for in my career up to now where large National company that would have a hierarchy and corporate structure that was very rigid in their organization. The approval process and workflow of projects had a path that was very specific and did not always accommodate my personal needs or approaches. The success of getting projects done required obedience to the process. The Obedience to the process had to do with understanding and accepting the process. My next lesson in leadership had to do with obedience, understanding, and accepting. Those three elements or what is needed to survive in a large corporate structure. Granted there are more elements, but these are considered at or near the top of the list in terms of importance. By focusing on some degree of obedience to superiors, understanding what is being instructed, and accepting the goals of the company will make and employee eventually become a leader in an organization. That works for me as most of my corporate life has been in the area of middle management.

Working in the corporate world in middle management with a staff assigned to me while at the same time I was assigned to a superior was a lesson in leadership. My belief is that the most difficult corporate position in a large National company is middle management. It forces a behavior of being humble as you report to a superior receiving instruction and correction while at the same time as a manager I had to issue instruction and correction based on what I had already received myself. There is the phrase that comes from the adage practice what you preach. Successful managers who are in middle management must do that if they are to be successful. Subordinates and employees may not realize it, but managers who are in middle management are constantly receiving instruction and continually being corrected to serve as a process of adjustment serving business needs. The lesson in leadership that middle management offers is primarily related to the behavior of being humble through the process of receiving instruction and correction. Management is a process of instruction and correction. That process can only be successful with the behavior of being humble.

Although being in middle management in a national corporate structure is an excellent way to build leadership skills, for me it was not the most profound experience in leadership. My greatest leadership achievement would only come by the launching of a business as

I started my path toward greater leadership as an entrepreneur. A business owner operates in a world of risk by taking Chances through faith that their goal will be achieved. My lesson in leadership as an entrepreneur involved my other previous learned lessons at a higher degree. I also learned the element of risk. The idea of risk men taking a chance with a possibility of the outcome being good or bad; positive or negative; success or failure. Only time passing up taking Chances wood develop the educated risk which in turn would reduce failure and increase success. That's called experience. An educated risk only comes from experience. Anticipated outcomes can only come from experience for it to be anticipated. That is why it's called an educated risk. Although a risk exists the educated risk allows for a more logical decision that would increase the probability of success and reduce the chances of failure. Leaders who developed this type of anticipation have developed experience overtime. Experience isn't something that is learned. It is something that is absorbed through the passage of time. I learned that leaders who have traveled through the passage of time have experience. As I write this, I have been an entrepreneur and business owner for 24 years. Given that, I have traveled through the passage of time that has offered experience that allows me to make educated risks with the probability of success being high and the chances of failure to be low that is proportionate to the experience of 24 years. The passage of time in the area of a quarter-century and beyond provide the experience that leads into and incredible decision-making process that holds logic and a high degree of success. I've seen it. I've earned it through the passage of time. I know it.

Experience is a very powerful tool in leadership that can only help the person who has the experience. I remember as a little boy that my father who was 41 years older than me try to embed experience inside me by providing knowledge to prevent failure. As a little boy that didn't work. I understand now that back then experience can't be given for it to be useful. It can only be learned through the passage of time. The knowledge that comes from wisdom is profound but can't be used to prevent mistake if the experience a failure doesn't. Although knowledge is important the experience are the train tracks that put knowledge to good use. This is called wisdom. Knowledge is what you know but the wisdom to put that knowledge to good use comes from experience. That experience comes through the passage of time. So, the effective use of knowledge comes from an experienced person. A person with experience will know how to use knowledge. A person who is without experience may receive the knowledge, but not know how to use it because they don't have the wisdom from the understanding that comes from experience.

Wisdom is knowing how to use knowledge because of experience earned through the passage of time. There is a process that happens before wisdom is in place. Wisdom is unique because it is not something that you can get off a store shelf. You can't buy it and you can't steal it. You must wait for it. Only perseverance and patience while doing the right thing produces wisdom. Given that, wisdom has it authority to be respected. Without the wisdom a person needs to submit and honor the authority that comes from wisdom. A duration of time and a passage of experience through a path of trial and tribulations graduates to a person at a level holding wisdom. That process hold authority and earns respect. It's not giving respect. It earns respect through the process of sacrifice.

Earlier I spoke about the difference between a man and a boy. The boy does to do in the man does must do. That was our discussion about responsibility. More recently I spoke about wisdom that comes from the experience of using knowledge over a passage of time. So there's been a discussion about different stages in people's lives. Perhaps I can be a little bit clearer of where people should be at to some degree. We'll try to outline it over the next few paragraphs.

A child is identified as one who lives at home. I'll use that simple to support the point that I'm trying to make. A child without the experience of true life challenges of living on their own typically does what they want to do and not what they have to do.

An adult lives away from home dealing with the experience of true life challenges. This includes a teenager wearing a military uniform willing to die for their country to support freedom for others. An adult what they have to do and not what they want to do.

A young adult does not have wisdom. They may have knowledge. They don't have wisdom that comes from the experience resulting from the passage of time using the knowledge that they have learned. That passage of time comes with mistake and discovery and revelation.

A middle-aged is young enough to have the energy to provide a contribution in the world they live in. That requires a good amount of energy. A middle-aged should have the wisdom from knowledge that comes from experience. Let me take a moment to say that again because it is so profound and important. A middle-aged should have the wisdom from knowledge that comes from experience. What does that mean? This is the time in a person's life that they should be setting forth their legacy. That legacy development can be the raising of children and getting them ready for college. It can also be a contribution to the world in other ways. Through a business. Through an invention. Through presentations via books, speeches, music production, film, etc. Whatever that contribution is will serve as a gift to the world and that gift is your legacy.

Beyond middle-aged is when the Legacy has meaning. The Legacy that is offered is a gift to the world. It is a contribution that has value. A person with the Legacy does not need to be the CEO of a multinational company. It can be a homemaker such as my mother who raised 8 children and offered them to the world she lived in. I am part of her Legacy because what I contribute comes from the seed she planted as part of raising me. And I am only one of eight. She has a huge Legacy. My father, in addition to raising eight children, discovered the atomic element hydrogen in space and launching the science of radio astronomy. (It's called the discovery of the hydrogen line) He has been called the father of radio astronomy by offering a window to the understanding of interstellar space and what is there. It allowed the mapping of galaxies. That is one of his legacies. A legacy is a mark or imprint that is left on this world because you were there. A legacy comes from leadership. What will your legacy be?

The result of leadership is legacy. Legacy comes from the activities of leadership in a person's life. Again, leadership is not just being a corporate CEO. I gave the example before of a homemaker raising children. My mother was a leader giving a legacy of eight children.

What will your legacy be? What are your plans over the next five or ten years? What will you contribute to the world you live in? What will be your mark or imprint that is left on this world after you go to heaven? What's next for you? What will you do? How will you do it? Who can you learn from who can you learn? Where will you get the guidance?

Be a leader and leave a legacy. You're in control. Take advantage of your resources. Being responsible. Manage your time. Take hold of the wisdom from the knowledge learned through experience. Set your course and direction toward the horizon of your legacy. Give yourself a chance for success because it is only you who will decide to move forward toward that success.

David K. Ewen, M.Ed.

Become a Leader with Authority
Your Success Toward a Legacy

Silver Anniversary Series

By David K. Ewen, M.Ed.

Copyright © 2018, 2019

Ewen Prime Company

All rights reserved. No part of this publication may be reproduced, distributed, or transmitted in any form or by any means, including photocopying, recording, or other electronic or mechanical methods, without the prior written permission of the publisher, except in the case of brief quotations embodied in critical reviews and certain other noncommercial uses permitted by copyright law.

About the book

There are many books and discussions about what leadership is. This book talks about how it is developed and what the purpose is through a person's life. By understanding the purpose of leadership, motivation is produced that lends itself to put people into the role of leadership. A leader can be a parent, a coach, a pastor, business owner, teacher, mentor, etc. This book gives insight and revelation to the power of leadership Behavior in a person's life to make them more effective so that they could leave a legacy behind in the world they live in before they go to heaven. Effective leadership gives purpose and meaning to life. Do it right and you'll be satisfied with having a purpose and honored for having a legacy.

37 - Become a Leader with Authority - **37**

Style of Book

This book was written as a narrative discussion as part of a lecture. This supports the silver anniversary series of Ewen Prime Company and is part of the celebration the topic of leadership is presented as in identifying factor of the success of the company.

About the Author

David K. Ewen, M.Ed. Is an author, speaker, talk show host, publisher, and entrepreneur. He has been seen internationally at education venues and institutions helping youth and adults maximize their potential through teaching and lectures. David is the founder of the Boston Institute for Business Leaders and Entrepreneurs.

www.ingramcontent.com/pod-product-compliance
Lightning Source LLC
Chambersburg PA
CBHW030039230526
45472CB00002B/586